ARCHÉ/ ELEGIES

E.D. BLODGETT

LONGSPOON PRESS

Acknowledgement is made to the following in which some of the poems in *Arché/Elegies* first appeared: *Ariel, Camrose Review, Contact Magazine, CVII, Dandelion, Heritage Magazine, The Malahat Review.*

Canadian Cataloguing in Publication Data

Blodgett, E.D. (Edward Dickinson), 1935-
Arché/elegies

Poems.
ISBN 0-919285-20-1

1. Canada - Poetry. I. Title.
PS8553.L62A85   C811'.54   C83-091166-9
PR9199.3.B596A85

Arché/Elegies has been set in Bodoni and in Univers 10-point type.

LONGSPOON PRESS
c/o Dept. of English
University of Alberta
Edmonton, Alberta T6G 2E5

Books may be ordered directly from Longspoon Press or through your bookstore.

Credits:
Editing for the press: *Shirley Neuman and Paul Hjartarson*
Book design: *Jorge Frascara*
Typesetting: *Cathy Schmidt*
Paste-up: *Jane Edwards*
Printing: *Co-op Press, Edmonton*
Financial assistance: *Alberta Culture, The Canada Council*

CONTENTS

How shall we speak of Canada,
Mackenzie King dead?

F.R. Scott

History, genealogically directed, does not have as its
ultimate purpose the rediscovery of the roots of our
identity, but, on the contrary, its unrelenting dispersion.
It does not attempt to find the centre of our being, the
first home to which, metaphysicians promise us, we shall
return; it attempts to bring out all the discontinuities
which dwell within us.

Michel Foucault

Epistre dédicatoire (prologue)

How many summers of the Iroquois
they stood, perfectly anonymous,
merely green, and nothing in their dreams
of Adam's late coming, slipping between
them, Adam, inexorable sailor sailing up
the blue and vaginal expanse, his mouth

a lexicon, his eye the eye of God.
For some, to be born is enough, to know the summer
sun in the green heat, the nameless beasts
running to no end in the infinite shade,
a music in the air without words,
knowing the fall of snow, unacclaimed,

unowned, only to fall, the kingdoms where
it falls but words, and everyone alert,
entering fables, their dreams monstered: o
to be reborn, all the stories new,
to run through far kingdoms, eyes charged
with myth, into invisible snow, the mists,

the virgin trees, instruments in hand!
Fable, astrolabe, and genesis
at last, one book and one law,
the trees of Hochelaga and Adam's eye
all one, the fables carried home,
everything exposed, the rest unsaid.

Arché! Arché!

Who would place a country here?
Aquí es nada, and God alone
would make something *ex nihilo:* how
do I utter the speech I enter entering you?
Where is the wind murmuring Beothuk
against the ship? How many soundless books
their black signs against the white of tongues
never heard again? Rubbish heap
of lexicons you are beneath your few
arpents de neige: no library
contains you, Canada, and what would it say
its narrow aisles aimed at silence? Roads

I have seen in Saskatchewan conclude so,
and so ending descry superb disdain
(Lorenzo de' Medici walking forever in spring
past willows and the bright sloughs, the dust
of buffalo blowing away, mysterious signs
of birds across the sky: to be there,
the golden hills of Florence all behind,
to ask, as the other poet asked, *"Chi è
questa che vèn?"* to see the clarity
of air tremble where lines of force
laugh at themselves, renascent, careless and wise)—

perhaps this happened once in Cree, its words
grave, speaking tomorrow from memory: to go
there we moved here, reading children
from shapes the birds took. Breath ends
and roads in gestures we could not foresee.
Even prophets fail, and wherever your hands
grope they touch the air speechless and
unread. Better to lose him—Lorenzo—and go
mute where words begin, where lines forced
into rock record, meanings speaking in stone.
I would be stone to begin again, and marked
in figures speaking: *kill, dance, eat.*

Origins

and exits lie dimly to hand: to part
as fish elliptically—elegant
Chekhovian poise—into ground, to lie
next to silence. How to speak, the earth
clogging your mouth, your eyes rooted with trees,
converted words? How to return, the place
making all going forward a door

flung wide, outside falling in—
the clearest songs of birds the open, air
itself apart, nothing that wasn't a door—
able to reverse the looking in
to praise, silence converting, eyes that turn
to God the open they enter, fish
moving dense within? Through this place

steps are periphrastic. To go out
doors swing in. Nature is
a room that leads to other rooms, the last
the room of solitude, Mackenzie King
inside himself. Who is to enter his
sentence unwinding, meaning running
out, all sense unhinged, words

that carry circuses, giraffes that stroll
through Saskatoon (the pomp, the acrobats
above Québec, aerial lines of words:
o, will they fall, the words in orange tights,
plains of words, words that leap from ground?)
brave metamorphoses, dominion, powers—
what *via negativa* wends entro-

pic thus, to see the open implode,
the swerve of origin, believing ends
are where place begins? Then speak the word
of Wolfe's suspense, his walk above the stream,
and tell me where to enter, words sur-
rendered, falling in parts as wounded fish,
the script intermittent, earth scored.

L'Anse aux Meadows, Newfoundland

Where was there **when** here? The fields go on
absently, looking over afternoon
into one sudden blue all random,
blue of forget, quizzical—fields asking,
"How is there any coming back to this,
to some shape of Thorvald, his name falling
on the stone shore, the birds rising so
awkward, dull-eyed, they are banned

from the long tales of wisdom, the bright surprise—
Thorvald, always coming after to find
his brother's track, all gone in the green
sea, to speak his own death, to hear
his name go slowly up with birds, away
and random?" I want to look at birds, their stone
translucent eyes falling into the **when**
of shores, no secret given up,

being stone, under foot. Where
is there any going from here, from stones their light
spent, a word unspoken? Why
do I pick them, thinking them blind, not stone,
making small heaps to shape a grave
place, walking into elements:
to see an arm dissolve, perhaps return
as fish, giving up against this

white space, refuse to write *Thorvald?*
Who else would take this revenge, turning
to silence, and turning silence into time?
So there is silence in spring. Ancient, it moves
Egyptian, regal, somewhat stiff—spring
as a shore bird, its track pedagogic and true,
the shadow proud. And silence coming back,
a renaissance that turns the air round,

awe concentric in hard, ecstatic places.
Who is to say, *What is gone*, the words traced
to sign, a grass that speaks parabola
and nothing more, complete Euclidean fall?
To write *Thorvald* there is only writing myself,
name signed in stone. And when did ships
glide upon the shore, in what spring
of what word saying *When I?*...

Pastoral for Parmenius

Green water world: to descend there,
to gaze at fish against the grassy banks
entranced, fish flocking to their far shepherd
singing of old Amphion breathing cities
beneath their mythic sky, and Thebes a song
of polyphonic walls, his lyre string
resounding through the speechless air, echoes

of dragon's teeth falling and falling across
the green sound; and singing of Hector's prime
and Hector's fall where once Achilles ran,
and singing of Jason's rocky voyage, and how
he entered Phasis and brought the magic back.
But what transfiguring of fish is this—
and what song, strange shepherd, did you

sail through, singing through that far
summer, plucking empires for a queen intact,
what song in the cold rain that fell
across the sea, through what time did you sail,
facing the banks of Newfoundland adrift
in fog, straining to sing your heroes' praise,
to hear the air grow dissonant

with cities, the trees abstract? Yet so you came,
and so saw the shore ambiguous
with stones, and the grey sea washing stones:
could you but speak, would you ask how they fell,
this sill of stones, what seeds they are and what
farmers come to harrow them to life,
and why the sea curls back to wash

as other seas on other shores where strange
feet struck earth, and songs unheard
rang terror in the air? And when will the rain
end, and is it the Flood and we the last?
Nothing is clear where even air becomes
sea, and skin almost scales. To leave,
to give the one body one is

up to water in a small ship called
Delight, burdened with dreams, a white ship
on a black sea, her wake a field of crimson
flowers, falling under wave—to leave:
how I would have stood on shore to bid
Delight God-speed, to call her back, to speak
into your ear your after words to friends

of heroes—*"et nos ama"* (love me, love
all farmers, all who cast their seed
of steel into earth)—to hear the fair
shepherd again, his song of heroes gyred
ever at sea. What have I now to do
but stand upon these fallen stones and ask
where *Delight* went down, brief sunset

in the eyes of Aztecs, spinning in stones of fire
through dark woods from sea to sea? Stones
(how much rain now must fall to wash
the stones wherever my feet seek earth)
stones, could they sing, their music would stun your ears
with dragon sound, no Amphion singing
cities uncoiled from his tongue, stones

settled, but stones entering your ears,
all lament inflected, renaissances
of sorrow, to hear the world anew as stone,
delight departing. So must you come back,
steeped in the green sea, to tell us: "Orphic
shade, sowing the hard, dactylic towns,
nothing but savage silences I seek

of fish, their mouths making the world one
passage from flesh to fish, bone spun
to sand, and I water, eating the walls
of cities, cropping shores, returned as rain."
Should Thales speak, the tales of stone rounding
off, his words as rain fall—so to speak,
to fill my hands with you, shepherd drowned

before your Arcady of Canada
choired in stone, I enter your rainy song,
calling into waves to summon back
your foreign tongue, your elemental flowers,
somewhere against these dry bournes to speak
water, become the sound of no word
bearing signs of a world water green.

Discovery   in memoriam Shanawdithit, *obit* 6 June 1829

I thought it only summer I entered—brief,
boreal passage—summer like ours, the same
year elsewhere, shadows falling from birds,
everything twilight—trees, the blades of grass,
birds of minor keys, even my hands
half light. I wanted it so to be
summer, a summer after Constable,
summer I could name, but not this

open before me, mirror of all summer,
crowns of trees beyond sight, and birds
their song falling to wet shade. I thought
between the trees and mute departure of birds
I saw my face, a focus of summer, the sun
splashed on my cheeks, and fish poised in pools
where I thought I saw my eyes. But what fish,
what eyes? I touched my face to feel

them there, seeking light, and felt my face
as something someone lost before my time.
But to see the fish frolic there,
to enter my eyes, to walk through my hair
as if the food were more delicate there!
Where can I go, my head so full of fish,
summer prey for birds, unable to speak
in this element of dust? I wish it well,

this face fallen from me, this shade once
mine. But to see it smile, my lips unmoved,
to hear it speak and say: "*Dyoot thouret*—
come down to me—I cannot see your face.
You move in air as a night-sun, an egg
afraid to fall. I want to see your eyes
and where you breathe and how you read the grass,
the sounds it makes, the various ways the wind

speaks. What is this word continually where
your mouth should be, trying to put a name
to me, a word so squared it falls closed
with no way out? I want you to speak my name—
ebanthoo, the place of fish—something you call
water in words of small drawers, words
where you put the sun away, words to hide
your face. O sun shadowed to pale stone,

where can I sit within these English words?
How can I say, my mouth running dry
with English dust, how deer came to drink
from me and bear fed upon my fish?
How my flesh grew hard when dark swallowed the air
and fish slept within me, haunted by dreams
of dry fire?" And heard it speak of death,
a surface fate, to float always between

water and air, element without
name. And looked again to see a plain
surface, shadows of no object, songs of birds
abandoned in sudden peripeties of fall,
clouds passing over water shaped
as fish. I must have reached some end of speech,
a margin of error, places of everything left

unsaid. Why are there no hysterical trees,
and how, having lost face, elision without
name, shall I enter this mute before of speech,
to move within the mouth uttering *grass*
here, to touch the green imperative
of spring opening earth and water verb
of rain. O mouth making grass, speak
into my eyes fish, speak face.

Leaving Louisbourg (N.S.)

Nothing lives here: even the birds
are cut from the sky—small kites, they hang
above a paper sea, their thin dreams
eyeing fish within the paper depths.
I fear the touch of stone, and fear the sea
where ships stand pressed against the sky,
ships I cannot walk around, ships

at bay where the birds scream, gazing down,
as I would want to scream, flat sounds
unrolling from my mouth, the words spelt
to echo something said in French, words
recalled, uttered outside, places where
grass grows from green to brown, and ships
lean under wind: o, the water,

what were the words for water? To call it forth,
to put it on, screens of pale green,
to see fish wakes streaming down your arms,
to dance wet in the streets, past fronts
of shops, the tower where the clock keeps pace
with times across the sea, to say: "Praise!
Praise the earth, the long arrival of green

realities of birds, the turning in arcs,
soundless curves in the opening air, the mute
reply of praise, its semaphore and shade—
praise in the walk of horses, praise in the trace
of rain falling, the deep praise of fish,
cosmos of roots praising earth, light
bending in space (quick dance of grass,

the dance of air)!" To hear figures arrive
applauding, the sound coming from their hands
of clapping written on the air, and up
beyond our small stage of France it goes
saying *louange* against the sky. I see
we are here forever, all speaking hung
within the air, cast off, nowhere to go

above the fort, the brief paper street.
I fear to say *farewell,* pretend we walk
the earth, to see whatever I say become
bird, blank sign in the dome of space,
absence shaped. I see there is no out
from here, but only in, reaching the sill
of speech—the awkward trees we see and ships

calling connotations in the air.
But what do they mean, the deathless ships, the trees
against the shore? How shall I speak them, their bare
shape, untouched, almost the sky? Do they wait?
Has something gone? How shall I say *They came?*
How utter France, how shall I start,
strung from word to word, to read back

from this sky, beyond the void where birds
are drawn, and images of houses where
the air is squared in glass? Teach me to breathe,
to open the fence of speech, to see ships
rise against the sky and birds return,
the emptiness of space closed: to breathe,
to move seamless into fire, forget

this bay of false starts, of grave suspense
where water at your feet falls dead,
where every rock, the coast and strange birds,
this house of marionettes, edge the sky
with proverbs. Teach me the things of speech, to speak
praise and hear flowers burst from my mouth,
lions leaving the air flagged in shreds.

Sculptor

Citizen King, you were right: the past
is ruin shaped; and now you have passed
to time's other place, some Kingsmere
so vast you have not seen those margins
where other kings pace, gazing within,
careless of music in the air, tambours
and broken breaths of flutes, small planets
turning in twilights, the solar fire snuffed.

Now you are gone, Mackenzie King. We lean,
some sad, against your walls. This is a house
not to be but to plan escapes. Where
are the chairs, the tables, the mirrors? How do we sit,
on what side of your past where straight ahead
is north, to take your fallen time in?
Are you the void above Elgin Street,
the void within the cenotaph, the void

within the wars, the soldiers staring up
beyond peripheries of blue? Perhaps,
Mr King, you were never but heaps of stone.
No need, Canada, now to turn
your ghosts free—none that is not ghost:
white plains of Henry Moores we are,
and now you see us all right through,
leaning as snow leans, edging void.

Métis

Speak the great names: Fort Qu'Appelle,
St Isidore de Bellevue, Grand Coteau,
Batoche, Fort Walsh, Frog Lake and Cut Knife Hill,
Seven Oaks and the rest of Rupert's Land,
and say what lies there between: bones
the wind gives back, bones of buffalo, bones
of the hunters, bones of Blackfoot, Cree and Blood,
the prairie piled white with hunts, all
bone brothers under sun. Name
me, Gabriel, king of this bare kingdom

of bones, riding and riding through white remains.
Name me, Gabriel, hero of the Wild
West of Buffalo Bill, hero of the great
Staten Island shoot out, me and Le
Petit, killers of little blue balls,
riding and riding through pictures of sage brush and sky,
fighting with clocks beneath the electric sun,
never as we used to fight, waiting,
talking, never arriving though miles and miles
of coulee and plain. And now where the prairie was

Sitting Bull and I and faces in the dark
square off, Chief of the great Hunkpapa Lakota,
dazed in the painted flats, and I, calling,
calling: God, will they find us, lost in faces,
before we stop forever, smiling in a glass
cage, where rivers stop, and birds hang
on the sky never moving? My smile is glass.
Everything lies inside me: buffalo run
to ground, streets I never saw where the elms
line faces singing white, singing

"The Stars and Stripes Forever," waiting for wars
and other shows at the town's end. They see
me, Gabriel, and see a war that hardly
was, a circus war so put off we almost
missed the last call. Dummies I gave
them to save my friends, men stuffed like the great
chief and I who drift slowly through places
and then through names where hundreds walk to gaze
and conjure us. Speak the names—me, Gabriel,
a clock ticking to an abandoned house.

Fall of Patriots

Papineau, Papineau, I seek the barest words,
their syllables in black, their faces stripped
and walking into ends of sounds. I want
periods that weep and words that break
against the ground, frozen, limping away
from mouths that utter them, gone to that

elysium of none to hear, the place
of lilies growing and blue uncertainties,
amid them Papineau, and walking through
the stubbled words Hubert Aquin, the seasons
winding down, another Ides of March
to see recede. But what does he hold, Hubert

Aquin, his palms up, surrendering all—
the alpine afternoons, topographies
of countries slipping into wakes, the days
without hope, falling, hour by hour
proffered to the ghost of Papineau,
falling where lilies their small counterpoints

of blue would dance, turning to sentences
he cannot think to end, neglect arrived
to reap the field? Could he have carried void,
the sentence that began at Saint-Denis,
suspended, gone too soon to seed, the crows
along the Richelieu entranced, afraid

of what their songs would say—the solitude
of words entering air, refusal of sound
and space taking shape, words that are
a leaving alone, and hearing them to see
a ground not wanting, orphans in heaps—
votaries of flesh—abyss reversed,

piece by piece emerging where lilies may
have grown, should Papineau recall, his eyes
harrowing void to dream? Do they embrace
across that fatherless abyss, and hear
the field moan, the sounds unsung
and rending fall, the harvest still to come?

O Canada

Country of no messiah, country of no
testament, country for whom there are
no seals to break: to speak your name
is to mouth gall, to utter *a-a-a*
and hear light crash in familiar streets,
the dust rising yellow beneath the sun

and faces crumpled in, bitter fruit
suspended on the autumn trees, mute
as lemons, fixed in cold decay, they look
straight ahead, wherever straight might be,
to find north, to pinpoint space, to put
something on the ground. Small towns,

stuck in fall, facing the air and sure
of where they are: to find them is how losing
begins, straying beyond maps, to look
somewhere under **Ca-**, perhaps, or other
sounds, mirrored gasps growing old,
frozen hiatus, spaced into solecisms

of slow expirations, winter's one
harvest. In this field the simplest words
deceive most: I want to say *the*,
but how do I stand to know where all that
finitude would rise, so precise
it stands, early winter unseen before,

a winter where **a-a-a** is no trick
of light, no dullness of lemons un-
remembered, no rot of small towns
choking air, but one beast of no
name, calling, untrapped by myth,
at large in absence of apocalypse,

standing over Saskatchewan its roads
stretching north to locate, to get lost,
to start decaying at four in the afternoon,
the year now forgotten, standing within
the space of lost heart and dead end,
calling, a merest **the** in an autumn of sighs,

wind in the small towns blowing, my arms
become tangents, and snow as space falling,
infinite end of seasons striking the void
of somewhere saying a, Lucretian sound
of snow intact. What place is this
of asymptotic skies, of white errata?

North

Where? where? where? terrible, brief
summer, wasps killing in the sun, apart
from Flanders, the place where no one eats the dead
but birds, aristocratic, heavy with forget:
had you but seen their eyes so serene
where the dead extend your seeing would become
knowing beyond all season. What

did you see, Thomson, and where beyond the lust
of wasps where you went not to return your skies
falling from the bright voids, departing from wars
we did not plan, skies stripped of birds,
skies so charged you must have bent double
to seize them coming down, framing death,
infinite, minuscule deaths where wasps

their jaws apart shred summer, all
light to flesh going away? But who,
in the end, never returned? It is we, and not
you, fixed in museums who stare always open
against walls, something entering us,
similitudes of knowing—this lake and that
other shape going up and bent, that place

where birds could not wait. Thomson, this is not
what you knew—it was the wind you could not stop
with your white boards, the ragged pines and shores
entering your eyes. This is knowing, when tree
and rock and wave all fall down,
tattered, your eyes no longer measuring sky,
but eyes riffled in the wind, old flags,

no one remembering. Is this what entered you,
Thomson, when we thought you had left the dying of summer,
seeping slow water, tangled in stumps,
apart from season, the small eating of wasps?
Are you perhaps crow, your knowing but dance,
turning in the infinite sun, your seeing gone,
serene, shredded, tree, rock, sky?

Explorer

Gone. Not one that asked which way was north.
What does it mean the south inverted so?
And some never spoke, gathering notes
in little books, rushing up the rivers,
away, their eyes open everywhere,
huge as lakes, no thing, no

hill, no emptiness beyond
that was not there reflected—flat, reversed
and floating past: so are Kelsey's eyes,
rhyming *fate* with *late*, to see his shade
always farther ahead and entering trees
days before he enters his notes, to see

fate, arrive and find it gone, always
too late, sight rhymes for a fiction unseen. Or other eyes, La Vérendrye's,
seizing the syllables of trees in French
where they speak, edging the wide shores with green
words, outlines falling apart at summer's end.

They are all—MacKenzie, Henry, Jacques Cartier—
maps of eyes, how many miles of degrees
falling cleanly through them, outsides marked
and put away, lakes whose surface lies
soundless, other, and all that's mirrored there
is wet—trees, canoes, hills and sky—

dripping from fingers moving away from south,
latitudes drowning wherever you take the world
in. Why do you ever come back, your backs turned,
gazing dully through strata and degrees,
to tell us, as Rupert Brooke would one day say:
"A godless place. And the dead do not return"?

How shall we sing the godless, the not yet
dead? O name the long measure of the world
where outlines lie before us on a page,
black notes against the white surveyed—
as one might turn north to music scored
for flutes, to rhyme *death* with *breath*, the air

figuring itself, proleptic and sure,
going always into itself, without
edges, no shade but lengths of light
refracted and still. Other music, the trees
transmuted to a speech of gods we cannot hear,
unwritten, grace notes without design.

Idylls of the King

I wanted to dream of small towns, and dreamt
of you, Mackenzie King. I wanted to dream
of skies that change, skies of early flowers
bursting over towns, and dreamt of blank
archival heavens, and you walking there,
walking through the void of judgements passed.
Mackenzie King, I wanted to dream of rain

falling as words of small stones within
my hands, speaking of how a town is made:
fences drawn through anywhere, a house
here beside my thumb, the distant sound
of hammers, roads crossing beneath a sky
of rain falling through a spring of flowers
saying *yellow*, and seeing **yellow** without

a word begin. I wanted to hear the sound
of stone. Wherever you walk, the small towns
emerging, the sky in self-absorption dies.
Why does the rain fall only on
your face? Why do I feel absence drawn
across my hand and hear pianos stop?
I thought I would see Sir Galahad beside

the road reborn, the rain falling, your eyes
spilling photographs against your cheeks.
I want you to open your mouth, Mackenzie King,
and say *mother*, to let the word warm
whole galaxies of sons revealed,
to speak through the going away of towns,
of curtains, the hang of absence. Tell me where

I will wake, wrecks of words dividing over
my hands. Tell me, what have you done to all
the towns, Mackenzie King, their flowered skies,
the rain in my hands? I want to see dust
in that place eternity is, to hear
pianos in my hands, the sound of stone.
I want to see you dead, Mackenzie King.

Our *Investigator* had the task of bringing Franklin's fate to light; in this she failed....

Johann Miertsching

Regina, Sask.

Why, when I sit in Canada, do I
hunch upon a pile of bones, of bones
so huge I must be entering mastodons,
walking through their seasoned ribs to brave
a death of no end, a souvenir
of death, and time that could not once have passed—
long seasons of flowers blowing so
minute across a plain, and mastodons

that drift through flowers unperceived, the beast
within emptied now to ice, distilled
somewhere to air. What kind of time is left
for mastodons but always coming back,
dreaming of death never quite arrived,
the time of Saint-Denys Garneau, his cage
of bones, a bird turning inside, his soul
hung from the bird's beak, bright flower

gone deeply to air? After Garneau,
who can be sure of birds? They enter us
at will, turning flesh to food, our bones
to cage: there is no telling all these sticks
apart where white against the ground there lie
the bones of Anne Hébert, *"reliquaire d'argent,"*
a life gone away and absence waiting
for death to come, as birds come back in spring,

beaks strewn with flowers unperceived.
Merely to speak is metamorphosis—
slight changes in the dreams of mastodons,
breath of antiquity beneath our skins
and prehistoric birds. There is no
entering of beasts that have not entered
other beasts before, stalking me, the bird
of Saint-Denys Garneau, *bouche fleurie.*

Sananguaq

No one forgot how cold it was, the air
crystal before them, leaning against its unmoved absence: whoever spoke, the words
cut into air signs of what our voices
sought, edging before us as names of what
was not, and there, through that absence, I

almost saw what no one knew to name.
But to see, only seeing through, what is
this, where something through summers never to come
came, and coming took all trace of us
away to nameless green, the buzz of space?
Have we become that, the disappearance

of words, gray plumes of breath, a shout
where a river forks, feet going away?
We could not see—was it the sky beneath
his feet where his tracks did not appear? And who
ran, his face rigid from sweat, crystal
and flashing it speaks, its words going mute,

going through the horizon of nothing to hear,
of white sinking, of animals moving somewhere
their long returns, entering eyes they come—
they destroy maps, they ford the hard stream
and the stream is gone where they move? After
is air, after is white. How many passed

there, I started to ask, but what voice
shaping words would reach that place
of dim entrance, that place that once
ran through heavy air, gagged with words,
animals crossing the stiff lines of his mouth?
Even silence falls apart, a piece

in time: what does it mean to translate all
these **afters**, the blur we saw, the speech
of huge beasts filling the air when he,
poised where the sun stopped, turned to call,
beasts upon his tongue, curved in their large
arcs, their answer deferred? I want to write

the simplest of words, to say how a man runs,
and how white comes down, and how,
now that he is gone, the snow sounds
and animals pass: through this—the snow,
the word, the man—what is this other, its
name lost, a line of silence left?

Sananguaq is the Inuit word for carving. *Sana-* denotes *making*; *-nguaq*
connotes *small, likeness, imitation, model, play.*

After A.J. Casson

What Ontario is this—alone
they all walk to our left, gazing
somewhere we have yet to see: a storm
falling through the north, someone gone,
perhaps at other yards to see still
others gazing left? How small to be

alone, Ontario squared, and someone out
of sight, gazing at us, puzzled that we
are not beneath a sky, no clouds
that stop against a frame, but somewhere enclosed,
not speaking, unconcerned with storms
we sit. Consider seasons into angles passing,

sides unseen so long that absence walks
beside them going nowhere—I forgot
their not being there, as storms without
wind. What did not pass is all they see—
absence of uncertain shape, surprised,
left behind the way pots of dead

flowers stand, giving no sign.
He tries to frame a question, the man I see,
to ask: "What do you see that moves somewhere,
unconcerned with the edge of things, beyond
the censure of sky? Is it how flowers look,
the air turned to colour, some so blue

there is no end to where they are?" But what
absence speaks? Absence is an air to touch,
surrounding your hand with old dust, and gone
it is all over—something you might store
apart, Ontarios saying, "No!" A shelf
closed in the sun, only corners left.

Photograph Archives

Someone speaks: it is a voice whose pitch
is never fixed—there are winds blowing through
it everywhere at once. You sit down
in any afternoon, in winter say
and late in 1921, to see
beneath your eyes a name never read

before. Whatever it is, a man perhaps
and lost, it runs in the snow on Dundas St.
The trams are caught in the early storm, feet
sliding in slush, black and white with shades
of gray, and everywhere within the room
the same mute clamour of names speaks

of what they were. I want to see the backs
of names, the sense they turn from, staring here,
never to doubt the blank space we fill.
But tell me, sitting here, what verb to write,
to speak of space that picks up time,
space inscribed as a Greek dance, a space

of 1921, *ex tempore*,
and Dundas St dispirited and cold
to tense provisos of grace turned round.
But why is there something always running out
of step in snow, never getting there,
a race of one foot always raised:

it means **to wait**, where nothing, not even trams,
achieves such poise, to rise above
the silence, black and white, of Dundas St,
leaping over 1921
to time, epiphanies reversed, a wind
of winter rushing in. O, to hear

it speak not dying, but how breath
without warning, negative departs:
"When is it?" it asks, this untimely wind,
seeking trees their leaf and root gone,
rounding a backless name, against my face
so cold I fear turning, to step in space.

Prairie Museum

You want to come running over sloughs,
past the small bluff of poplars, bluff
of five trees, their leaves almost gone,
to see them final—five ecstatic trees—
running past sloughs, the late ducks,
the trees. You want to come running near
the sun, unable to see the sun burning

there, but clean fire, and sloughs turned
back to rain, and rain mothering all.
But to come past sloughs, the yellowed grass
along the shores, what entrance now
to this bare shell of solitude:
His Majesty before the War—he smiles,
you would not think the war would come, yet so

it came, and still he smiles. You want to hold
the solitude of smiles, Riel's pipe,
to find solitude itself beneath
the letter *s*, whole as an apple, as
one would seek *sod* and *slough* and *skull*,
silence and *Saskatchewan*, filed
the way one files breath, each ex-

halation gone and coming back restored—
a pot of John Chalke, to hold the air
of all loss in place, the loss of all
but things unsaid, the silence never made.
What is the entrance to all that loss, of things
that have not found their words, of things beyond
the ecstasy of poplar bluffs, the world where you run

in one place, apocalypse and shade,
and things you have not seen returned and put
away as *s*? But what places, what
other words to stand naked as trees,
gazing wherever you run, the sun turning
farther into fall? You want to run,
and where to run, the trees timeless and sloughs?

Havdalah   for Bender Hamlet, Manitoba

How did it get here, from where, this afterthought
of all *shtetl* whose name no one knows:
it makes the silence tilt, and where glass
opened the wall, only wind and scraps
of white move. Who is there here to read
this white absence, to say "the air

was never void—everywhere it moves
slick with *luftmentshen*, dancing through rain, through sun,
moving the air you breathe through seasons you
have never seen, and when they speak, these absent
children of air, the world you would see turn
sabbath beneath their tongues, and what few

trees were there leafless after fall
would burn, branched with candles: whoever walks
here, enters absence, apples falling,
wine flowing over prairies, somewhere
the air opening Chassidic with song,
walls blown away, no edge

of white behind calling **defeat** through miles
of space, piercing absence, calling through
centuries no one names"? What are the sides
of silence, its inside of old chairs, seats
broken through, wherever silence breaks,
and faces on a wall gazing where

wine might have flowed, prairies singing
in their sad tongue, singing the sun's return,
the air's hilarity? Who stands in the words
they speak, music like water on your skin,
breathing green sabbaths, an air cleft
with leaves of grass, ground bass unbound?

Havdalah (Heb.: *separation*) marks the end of Sabbath. A *shtetl* is a hamlet.
Luftmentshen is translated in the text as *children of air*.

Returning to Busby, Alta.

After we put the rest of Georges Bugnet
to ground, walking apart beneath the blue
and static sky, I found myself along
the road to Busby, white going away
past the lake and old, arthritic trees,
beyond the coyote staring in the field

of white at me along the road against
the fence—myself, my eyes open, complete
with solitudes untouched by wind, the clear
distance of solitude, a shack before
it leans in time, the scentless air, a **then**
of no forgetting, pristine solitudes

of winter 1905 taking stands
within my eyes. Wherever I saw you old,
enclosed in rooms that age sits through,
wherever you were, immobile, panes of snow
hedged us inside, the yard through the window set
wherever now would be. Perhaps that is all

the **now** there is—angles of white roof,
ends of old grass against a wall,
flawless shadow waiting for time to come,
a time for coyotes, watching, uncertain yet
where to move. Do coyotes sit with us,
unseen, edging the margins of 1905,

coyotes entering glass, the walls of light
between us and now? It is enough to ask
questions of fences, speaking of coyotes so,
walking into Busby, the store closed,
clouds suspended in glass, a long cry
in the air and silence as grass bent to ground.

House in Saskatchewan

So sure they are, hard against
the sky: to ask *where*? is gone away,
and whose feet move within the dirt
you forget, the one tree beside the house
a sign saying *tree* through each leaf.
It looks nowhere, a sign that does not ask:

to enter such houses an unknown script
comes apart, whatever wrote *tree*
running back from tree and green leaf
before the field, the sky and house became
the place you see speak. To take a step
you feel brushed in, turning clear

Chinese beneath a sky saying no more
but *sky*. It is you at last translated here
within the house beside the tree. You want
to ask how dust dying sounds, to see
the shades of words spoken here fall
across the room, but even shades are gone,

a pot left, abandoned on the floor,
speaking of no loss, taking the light
in, open on the floor, and nothing in
the room not moving toward it, saying
empty, wherever you look—the door, the light,
the tree refusing all after, all

before—transparent, speaking always place
as proverb. You want to ask of going, what
it means, and open—where it is, and where
you have gone, entering Saskatchewan.
You thought an essence passing by you touched,
your hands become word, being spelled.

Going Through Craigellachie

Put it away. A box of pins would hold
all of it, the sound of men against
the ground, weapons given up, the tears
of widows drying, children walking round
and round till death comes and they forget.
Put it away, its syllables of rites,

its game of unforgetting in the long rooms
where anything red—the late sun fallen
into peaks, autumn on the face of streams—
grows timeless, the stories repeated word
for word until the trees, the high rocks
spring from the ground of words. What did they sow,

singing their tales of how things came to be,
but words across the earth, words of hard
edges, mountain crags of words, telling
change, how once they took the shapes of men,
how dying they stood against the mountains, green
and carrying the wind? Put it away,

this hard ending here. If Craigellachie
were a word to say *eyes*, they would be blue,
the colour of snow toward the end of day,
not deep, but long, ending in icebergs. If
into that snow you suddenly chose to walk,
what kinds of caravans, lost camels

in that frozen gaze, what dreamt departures,
what Franklins always staring farther, small
remains heading nowhere, white ships
but schemes against the sky their secret lost,
what would you meet, and what to say, and where
to follow, camels moving slowly through

the passes? Of dreams we die, Craigellachie,
where each for someone else is poised, then blurs,
then seems to vanish, camels walking through
us into dark. We die of words, we word
death. But so the trees and rock emerge
from words ending in ground, the speech of earth—

mute, no one to fathom, talking of where
ends meet, out of sight above
the ground. It speaks of endless camels, long
hosannahs of camels falling from our mouths,
wandered where perspectives cross, journeys
going through themselves, to vanish, arriving

speechless in the strange gorges. What do we want
them to say? To bless the wind, to turn green
geometries to music, children as pure
notation singing, singing, the air translating
Allah? But what speech, what opens us,
no sudden end of flesh against the air?

Invisible Country

Queer little birds, their feet tied
to strings, and out, beyond diastoles
of cloud, the gods sit, a childhood
upon them, all light, and songs always
beginning, spring at their feet as fresh grass
(and what colour would childhood possess
but green, translucent, unperturbed, to be

the one idea of childhood of green,
no other colour known?) nothing yet
recalled, before time somewhere teaching
white nostalgias, the snow looking back,
their gaze upon the light girding space
before wonder, no one remembering first
surprise, Ovidian April before Aprils

came and went, unison gaze of gods
descending into clouds and into the feet
of birds upon a string. What charm
is this, to look north, against the high
immobile *mise au point* of birds, to hear
one say: "I never saw the place but saw
the trees, their unfulfilled, the birds beneath

the clouds, their gazing out, suspended from
the noosphere of gods, divinity
of gas, and never heard the air come down
with song falling from the rigid beaks
of birds, or leaves appear upon a branch,
but fruit abstractly hang, pears that dream
of pears becoming pears, and stillness as

a law. O, Adam again, and Adam's friend,
beneath a cloud you stand, the air you breathe,
your bodies that do not recall the fruit,
o, almost elements, what place is this,
no roads but allegories screened against
the sky where figures wail and signs fill
the air, Delphic **e**, letter to spell

Eden, memories of wars and gods
vanished in sudden rains?" Speak, Adam,
the literal air, sentences that seek
the broken shapes of leaf, the rain that runs
against the possible of trees, the birds
to find the speech of song, the sky unstrung—
Adam gazing, speechless at birds in their fall.

...faintly the inimitable rose.

Light Verse   for Hannah Maynard (and other photographers)

The pure dance of surface, the move of absence—
what is the place of names, to say *rose*
(its shape against the page), the pure you seek,
its stepping forth from void? It must be behind,
the turn of dancers turning, to become spiral,
all body, exfoliate, leaf
of space, leaf to be held against your skin,
leaf fallen to vein, negative

of leaf and circling up to winter, dust
of something else, of no one a rose, to hear
its voice of no one again say *open*
and see the open falling wherever you look—
to see **down** going further in
until a balance strikes. To speak of such
joy, entering where dancers are,
centre empty of itself, the in-

spired turn: o sacred offering
of breath, eternal Manitou, the voice
revolved, the axis turning emptiness
out, my skin an absence to wear! I fail
to speak of you, your face in shade, a word
enveloped, undisclosing, unable
to take the letters off, reveal the word
in negative, the light arriving, re-

verberation against the blank shore.
From where does dark come to gaze across
a spit of sand and take water in,
a figure closing the farther edge, the dance
repealed, the rose of no one stopped? To de-
scribe: the dancer goes away, the thread
of light unspun, no other sun the same,
unavoidable, a rose upon her toes.

Colloquy in Fall

Somewhere north of Ottawa, the road
branched to fall, no longer sure how going
back would be, the brief towns, the lakes
falling one by one apart, mere
image, a light unrecalled, to take
all forgetting away. How many trees
must rise somewhere inside me, Ottawa
its road leaving it behind, the shade

of old Mackenzie King, perhaps myself,
who spoke beneath the trees, the words falling
from his mouth you would have thought them leaves
so slowly they fell, uncertain where to land,
to take forgetting away. "From where?" I cried,
the question as a sudden gust disturbing,
no other sound to hear but that autumnal
silence, similes of void that fall

within the shade. What is the way back
from here, through what reflection of leaves,
past the trees, another outside
(and what to call it, country beyond trees
where Sibyls never spoke?), an afterdark
not falling under leaf, your mouth
so filled with leaves you could not speak for dust?
Then you are done, no sooner flesh than word

for someone else to speak, reflected, dreamt
perhaps, when those who disappear come back
to mind. Do not speak to me of where
Dumont has gone or what became of Saint-
Denys Garneau, to hear the echoes here
of leaves resound, of words within a baffle
calling to themselves, last words
of someone slowly put to death, a room

of words choked off, and then screams,
and finally sounds you never heard—of stars
when they collapse or planets listing within
perpetual fall. No one is ever alone
but thrown with bones and bones of words, and you,
Mackenzie King, and I, the words we were
shifting through the pitch of planets, ca-
dence of eternal choreographies.

Totem for Emily Carr

She sits, autumn falling at her feet—
old season, old feet. She sits,
eyes fixed in autumn, leaf dust
sifting: I want to touch her death, to walk
through leaves decaying, the aura of dust
breathing the air almost giving voice.
She sits, her face of no end speaking

into dust, her face of slow inflection
about to become sign, forgetting, turned
back, place where words collapse. Where
is the death I had to touch, and where am I,
a place in autumn, my back against the sea
and friends lost on the strange shores walking
over sand, the huge wall of forest

shut before my eyes? What is it for,
this green abyss of speech, impossible
losing, mute raven compelling what
praise? Even my fingers refuse reply,
unwilling to touch the air, alphabets
and what they spelled adrift, to pass sign
after sign no sooner seen within the air

than gone, giving up, history lost
at sea. I fear to say *open*, to ask
where, to see direction disappear,
your face rifting from leaf to dust, to turn
unmoved, no north, the great sea I crossed
falling in, the earth dry, nowhere
left to move, all horizon turned

to sand. What kind of ending is all this,
the stories that we knew unravelled,
a face reversed, a language looking back
to find its letter **a**, to undeclare,
elegies losing, to exhale all,
the air breathing, about to say *ho-
liness* and stopped short of saying more

than *o* breath turning round itself,
fish almost appearing, nothing yet
revealed, the air unfathoming?
Who would be there to see the rain fall,
to read the terrible thrust of green, her face
of no outside, raven decaying, raven
become tree, taking breath away?

Epistre dédicatoire (epilogue)

Here is losing: that we hear the wind speak,
that we say the heat is green. What map is there
to say, "Silence is an after of words?"
To sit with words at one's feet, all the streets
changed, buildings broken, kicking glass—
but the great river we knew, whatever god
within, and somewhere after the trees the gate

of dreams, the ivory metamorphosis,
ending, ending in light, o Eden, o
golden always falling after trees!
And so this book of giving up, better
reduced to syllables, morphemes heaped
against a shore, than this coming to end
in word, wherever we look the sun turning

to myth, hanging from astrolabe and poem,
drifting into Heisenberg, the sun
unsure, its never rising again perhaps
perhaps. . .
            How, then, believe that this was more
than going into elliptical dream, going
out almost and almost coming back,
as suns that disappear almost, leaving

the cosmos endless, fable never to finish,
a sun of silence hanging inexorably
in space unnamed—but even to unname,
approaching to say, "There are no names for this,"
to send across the vacancy of space
more epithets for God Who hides within
the sun. . .
            Teach me, whoever you are, to walk

backwards, to take this ellipsis, this
double *is* as all there is, words
looking in to end and looking out
to that place they would not reach, words
as innocent as beasts that gaze, the world
its silence absolute, necessities
of **sun** and **moon** unsaid, their cosmos turning

where beasts walk, eyes burning joy,
their long burdens of silence carried within
their elements of air and water and earth.

I fear to say this, to give you beasts
that mean, beasts to hear with astrolabes
of sound, to hear suns in their eyes, to put
words, awful finalities, into your mouths.

Anagoge

For James Wright (1927-1980)

1

This last walk I take with you,
moving past trees you never saw
before, through tracks of green abstractions and air
unspoken. I want to ask just this:
where have you gone, always walking before
me, walking through the small Ohio towns,
other towns—towns so other you knew

men who had seen trees that. . . But why speak
of trees now? Where you walk there are
no trees, your hands slipping into signs,
seizing speech yet to come. I took
this walk to find you somewhere I had been,
and where did you go but east where the sun comes
sooner, a light of clear sound. I took

this walk continually walking farther west
thinking: "now he will say 'Luke Havergal'
again," and the silence opened with sparrows, glass
falling. How do I enter this broken space
of song closed with no song at all?
My eyes slipped with tears: blades of grass,
an air thick with flowers—even trees,

to after-songs of sparrows all changed,
the dark cut clear. None there is
to say *Ohio* here, but why speak?
Here horses begin their long dream
of fall, horses dreaming history, blades
of empire blowing westward to the sea,
history so reaped within their eyes

you'd say: "now kingdoms sleep, time
is an old woman and here it is always late
afternoon, she is pale green, she becomes the sea,
the pace of slow horses carrying fall
away through the sleeping kingdoms, white towns
of Ohio, twilights of sparrows—the sea
is an old woman, I want her to speak of fish,

the dark that fish know, the speech of fish
rising to the air of coasts where I have walked
breathing the language of fish, the air splashed
with laughter, an old woman, pale green—
mother, the sea, Li Po—I swim through airs
of green song, my body speaks fish."
But what shall I say, now that you are gone?

2

That you are fish, that we must sit here
against a shore of space and believe now
tales of old wives, listening to waves
falling, spacing silence? Do you believe,
now you have left us our kingdoms sound asleep,
your old Ohios, your tales of horses so
wise they yawn and towers topple, streets

flood with fire, small children in the air
as fireflies tossed in the summer nights
bright and gone? To believe this you must
believe what gods tell themselves to while
away time watching mortals play,
believing what we cannot bear to know—
that even generals do not speak but are

spoken through, that **green** was never said
by us saying *green*. Is this the speech
that you put on, walking wherever you walk,
origin of summer beneath the thin trees
I pass? I breathe, then, empires their slow
collapse and how many children now gone
to air and sudden light. Knowing this,

"Puedo escribir los versos más tristes esta noche,"
knowing you have not been but passage, a man
speaking words to become how words begin.
That you might have been, and where, I cannot say:
without an end, nothing begins—we are
the grass we walk through, the fire we fear,
the horses that dream us, the words the gods use

to pace their immense forevers. What is there now
to forget? I took this walk to find a man
I barely knew, to make him come to life,
to stand somewhere under trees, revealed,
to say perhaps what rain is, falling,
to be himself, beginning, saying what is,
speaking air. What is there now to forget?

So Ohio becomes fish, complete
with all there is to know, mortal as grass.
What other fields are yours, friend beyond
recall, and have you uttered what you are
at last, and what are the words, what sounds
we cannot shape—there where proverbs walk
stately as horses, eyes old with farewells?

Postscript:
about Archaeologies

"Je suis un renard," dit le renard.
　　—Saint-Exupéry
(Car JE est, etc.)

Several years ago, Isaiah Berlin published
a marvellous little book *The Hedgehog and
The Fox.* Its point of departure is a fragment of
Archilochus that reads: "The fox knows many
things, but the hedgehog knows one big thing."
Then, without pressing the limits of the defini-
tion to a point where any writer or thinker
might escape, he suggests that Dante would be
a hedgehog, while Shakespeare would be a
fox. The distinction cannot help but provoke,
and I have often wondered whether I, not
daring to include myself in the company that
Berlin argues might be either all-enclosed,
centripetal, or going off in every direction,
were like the hedgehog, hunched and prickly,
or like the fox, prone to ruse, sniffing out the
possibility. I think the former comes nearest,
asking one question, no matter how much the
accent shifts. One runs, of course, a risk or two.
A hedgehog is untidy, and not one to attract
poetry. But hedgehogs also call to mind electro-
magnetic fields, the kind made visible with iron
filings for spines. Move the magnet, redesign
the field. That, at least, is an appealing hedgehog, capable of translation.
　　Berlin did not, however, consider the
hedgehog moving somewhere, in a forest of
darkness perhaps, where foxes continually
take the shape of words whose moves always
possess some cunning attempt beyond the
reach of mere hedgehogs. If it were not for
words, russet flashes of words, the accomplish-
ment of the hedgehog's single intent would
move instantly (how could it be otherwise?)
from poem to trance, and Dante would never
have been known other than as rose, a rose of

fox: scof (f)

or muse
Deleuze

read a
sign

'edge 'og?

eternal turning, no rose that flowered suddenly in an Italian summer of 1300. But if the time of foxes were only historical! We would think that once we had passed one it would not return, slipping behind us into centuries and into sounds we never heard said. But trapped in time they are, nevertheless, free, and those left yesterday await us in some tomorrow, some dark turning. Curious labyrinth of lost intent: if a fox can become word, so can ants, spiders, birds, horses, and hedgehogs. This is a transformation that is, at last, a surrender. What is the word that hedgehogs, forgetting, become? For me I thought it enough to say *I*, purely and simply, the way one always, never taking thought, says "I," as if, whatever the word

I
re-
lie

meant, it could always be relied upon to be in place like an ear. It is not wise to believe that even hedgehogs are as reliable as an ear, and ear is as reliable as hedgehog in a forest of foxes. With such words "ahead" and such "behind" an ear is a doubtful messenger. How can I tell what it makes up, whispers to me for the sheer joy of playing with foxes all night? And what unthought relationships are hidden in that odd pair of words, "I hear"! What happens to this thing of one centre, this hedge-hog I call *I*, always attuned, and always on the

one
un-
done

verge of losing tune and tone, unsung, one song? I would sooner articulate a silence.

It was such an illusion to think that if a word could be seized at its beginning—pure Greek, pure Cree—that its elusion could be tamed. But what beginning? The movements themselves of animals are already figures, and the first movement, in what arcane silence, must have been a trope. As honesty becomes a hedgehog, I would rather stand at the other end from beginnings, pretending to gaze to-ward them, somewhere "behind." No end of figures there, and hedgehogs transformed, not

I'm
prim-
al?

always looking like other hedgehogs, palimp-
sests of former hedgehogs edging into primal
tropes, hardly imaginable. But as a poem is a
figure, so a primal trope is not a beginning but
a centre, a place where the poem tries to refer
itself. Is this what I meant when I said of Kelsey
in "Explorer" when his shade was seen as fate,
"always/ too late, sight rhymes for a fiction
un-/ seen"? Where else would such seekers
walk but through an "air/ figuring itself, proleptic and sure,/ going always into itself"? That
is perhaps why in "North" I could not find Tom
Thomson but in "similitudes of knowing". Even
that is not a failure. And what is left of that
other strange wanderer, Stephanus Parmenius
Budeius, but water always seeking word, and
figuring so many other poets, their dreams
charged with a danger and a beauty they cannot read before them?

So I have wanted to call these poems, of
which these three are emblematic figures,
"archaeologies": not because they are "about"
beginnings (**archē**), but because they seek the
figure (**logos**) that deceives us, by making us
believe that the figure we seek may echo some

o
echo
re-
see-
d

primal figure, itself another echo, receding into
silence that is neither ending nor beginning.
Such a hopeless task this would be if I were in
pursuit of the past or if I thought that beginning
was other than figure! Why must "past" always
be behind us? Surely we know the past, surely
we are the past, figuring a past for someone
else. As a hedgehog, in fact, one must be a
centre for foxes, designed to articulate their
figures. So, I see, I have asked of Thomson,

a crow
would know
so

"Are you perhaps crow, your knowing but
dance?"

But there is no ending with Thomson,
wherever ending is, nor with archaeologies, the
speech of endless escape. The end is turning
in, inchoate tropology of words no sooner said

than casting forth a past. To sing, then, beginning itself, farewells already figured before us,
hastening to summon into sentence what might

o
Papineau,
no!

have been before it was—is that to say *o*, our
sentence taking itself in: to be words in sub-
stance, spoken and speaking, a sentence
shared, and silence but waiting to be uttered
again, the round force of our calling back an **o**
in long echo? Is there, and should it be asked,
a Canadian sentence, and how long would it
last? No end in sight, it is the sentence of endless arrivals and endless elusion, the sentence
that cannot end, always condemned to seek
itself without recognition, the sentence that
laments its own losing. What else can it do but
leave itself forgotten in its own track, speaking
to itself of itself, its first word already calling
what is to come, and calling whatever follows
back. The Canadian sentence is shaped to

re: re

resume, yielding forever to the illusion of beginning, continually passing through that place,
an end in itself. It is a hedgehog on the track of
a fox, arch-sign, russet going to ground.